To Julie
with best wishes always —
Karen Fowell Koenig
Christmas, 1993

Sacred Process

Karen Koenig

Kärelek Press

Cover: *Self-Portrait* by Karen Koenig
oil, 20 x 23½ 1988

Library of Congress Number 93-078581

ISBN 0-9637203-1-7

Published by Kärelek Press
800 West End Avenue #14C
New York, NY 10025

Produced at The Print Center., Inc., 225 Varick St., New York, NY 10014, a non-profit facility for literary and arts-related publications. (212) 206-8465

Table of Contents

This book is dedicated with love to my children,
Cami, Michael, and David.

Heartfelt thanks to Steven and David, without whose love and support this book would never have come into being. Deepest thanks also to all of the people, seen and unseen, known and unknown, whose hard work, good wishes, caring thoughts and prayers have helped me come this far.

Karen Koenig

"There are as many ways to pray as there are moments in life.... In all these moments, you gradually make your life a prayer and you open your hands to be led by God (the Spirit, the Unseen Reality, the Numen) even where you would rather not go."

Henri Nouwen
With Open Hands

Introduction

My wife Karen has enjoyed doing art all her life, realizing from the age of twelve that she had a mysterious gift for creating a likeness. Her career as an artist began with portraits of her three children in 1972. As time passed, she grew increasingly active as a professional portrait artist. Examples of her work appear in this book. As her children became older and more independent, art filled her life with ever-greater challenges, enjoyment, and satisfaction.

In 1966, three months after the birth of her third child, Karen discovered that she had von Hippel-Lindau disease (VHL). This is a rare, genetically transmitted disorder, which affects primarily the eyes, brain, spinal cord, and kidneys. In its later stages, it can be devastating to any part of the body. VHL began to affect her eyes more than twenty-five years ago, and she eventually lost all sight in one eye. But it was not until January, 1992, that impairment of vision in her only seeing eye ended her career as an artist. It was out of these circumstances, and with the encouragement and guidance of my poet brother, David Koenig, that this book came into being.

Steven P. Koenig, M.D.

Preface

My sister-in-law Karen Koenig's verse does not originate from a schooled or trained poet. Having written only occasionally until fifty years of age, this talented painter who could no longer paint suddenly began writing flowing verse. And what miraculous verses these are, you are about to see. Her unique, unusually pure and natural voice constitutes her greatest strength.

This voice emerges from a place so deep in the heart—in such a deep heart—that even the most honed poetic tools of the most well-known poets rarely reach that place. Her illness has been the instrument of her poetic education…her guild, her crash academic course, her professional initiation. Like the poetry of those throughout the ages who, seeing death at the door, have begun to write verse, her poems possess urgency, intimacy, and truthfulness.

And yet, Karen Koenig's voice is often wryly humorous, consistently positive, always spiritual. Her verses are not about dying as much as about living. Whether the reader is one suffering from a disease, or well in body and simply experiencing the joy, trouble, and eventual dying that every life brings with it, these verses are a guide to courage—to valuing and coping. They reflect a life lived with remarkable integrity, dignity, and joy. They are a revelation and irrefutable proof of a beauty and ultimate order of life that no catastrophe—not even illness and death—can destroy. Of Karen Koenig's *Sacred Process,* the triumphant words of Dylan Thomas ring truest: "And death shall have no dominion." Thomas, at the age of twenty, defined poetry as "The expression of the unchanging spirit in the changing flesh." (Letter) At over fifty, Karen writes:

Farther along,
I now see
The Process
More thrilling,
More exciting,
More awesome,
More joy-inducing, delightful
Than ever.
It approaches
Rapture.

(Sacred Process—As I See It Now V)

David Koenig, Ph.D.

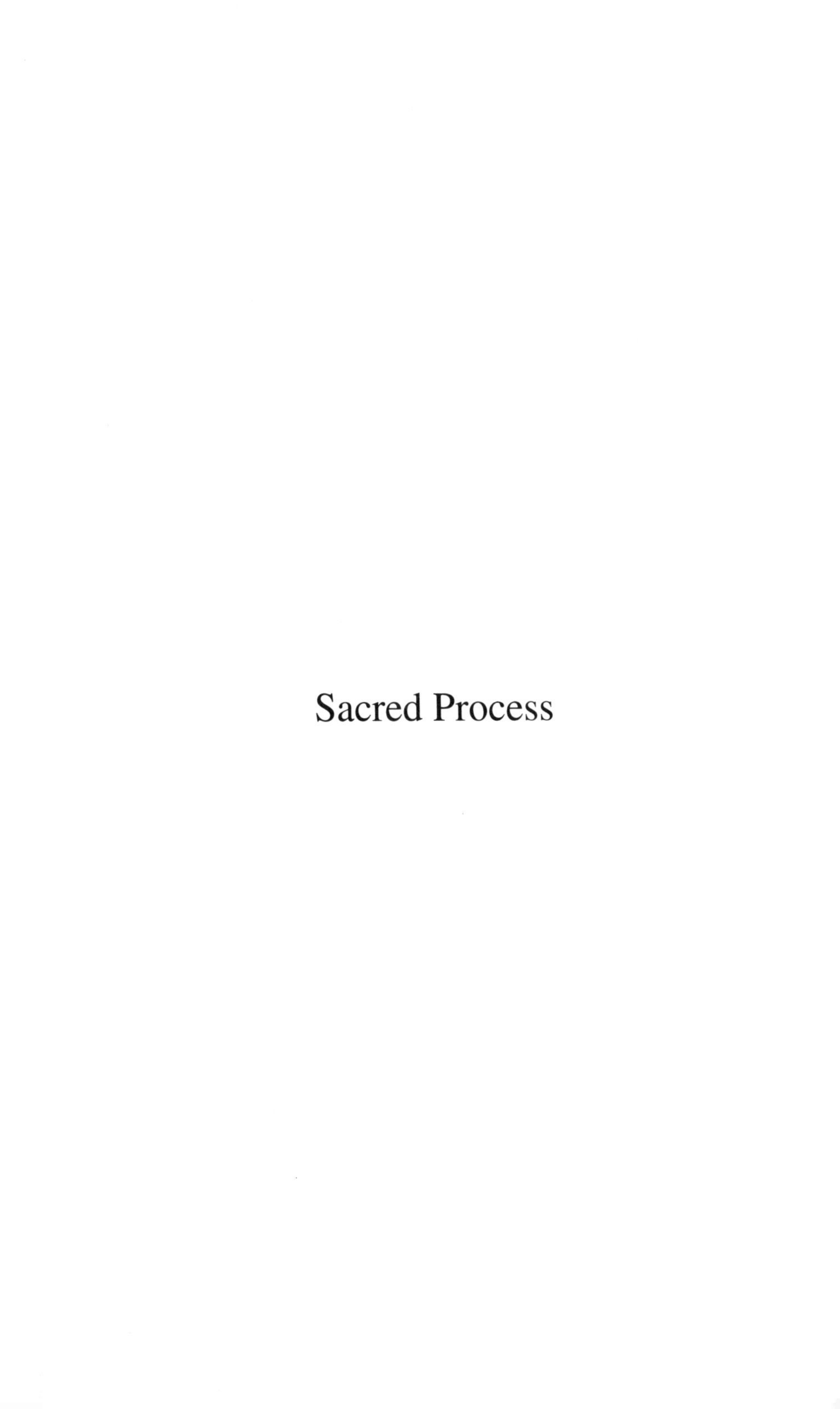

Sacred Process

Dear Steven

May 21, 1991
On plane home from Europe
with my daughter

Dear Steven,
Thank you for being my partner
In the continued effort
For a peaceful, healthy home.
I am convinced
Our struggle is blessed.
It means the world to me how
We push on,
Together and separately,
To understand our pasts
And come past them.
We've come a long way already,
And will continue, I hope,
For a long distance yet together,
No matter what the future brings.
I love you forever,
Dear husband,
Dear fellow traveler.

I Thank God
(For Steven)

December 8, 1991
2:15 am

I thank God
For skies and trees
And gentle breeze,
For rabbits, bears,
For joys and cares,
For ice
And mice,
For vegetables and rice,
For you
For me
For I and thee.
Life here's the best—
We are so blessed!
For merriment and sorrow
To share today, tomorrow
With YOU—
For this
I never really stop
Thanking God.

Soaking Prayer

December 8, 1991
3:30 am
After my sons' surgeries, 1991

Soaking prayer
Seems to be what's in order here.

I feel like
I'm standing chest high in the ocean
And the wind is picking up velocity,
Coming off the water.
Each wave crashes on the rocks
And bashes me.
It takes every ounce of energy to stand erect,
To hold on to the shifting sands
With desperately curled claw-toes,
And not give way to the overwhelming power of the water,
The rising tide,
The ever-swifter undertow.

How long can I hold on?
Can I make it back to shore?
It seems too far.
The thought of just relaxing, giving in,
Crosses my mind with increasing regularity.

"Choose life," says Deuteronomy.
Says Heschel, "Just to live is holy."
But perhaps there is more to life than meets the eye.
Could it be that there is another leg of the journey?
After tide and energy ebb,
Will there be an easier place to go?
Another place where I may, peaceful, flow?
I love the thought of heaven, always have.

I'll soak in prayer then. By and by
I'll find the deep, still place where answers lie.

I Feel Like a Wild-Eyed Doe

December 8, 1991
3:45 am
After Mike's diagnosis and surgery

I feel like a wild-eyed doe.
All deer know
That there are wolves out there,
But life goes on.
We do our best
To be alert,
To be careful,
To use all of our wit and instinct
And when danger swoops in close,
To fight, fight!
Use all of our strength and resources,
And to hopefully fend off the peril.

When we're young, agile and strong,
And when we're only needing to protect ourselves,
Evading the threat is a relatively simple thing.
But now I have a fawn—no, two—in danger!
And the wolves are close, menacing.
I hear their stealthy moves toward us now.
The tiniest crackle and rustle tell me they approach.
My heart pounds.
I strain to be ready
To protect not just myself, but now my babies.
I see glowing wolf eyes,
Their gleaming fangs!
I rear up on hind legs
And find a roar in my throat
Which I never before knew to exist.
My precious young, huddled in the thicket,
Get up on shaky legs to run/resist.
The predators bound toward us, leaping.
I rear up, eyes bulging,
Hoofs flashing, thundering.

Can we survive?
Will all we have to fight with be enough?
How much will we have
Of ourselves or each other
When this onslaught
Is over?

Hardships Are Blessings

December 8, 1991
4:30 am

I see health and illness both
As inescapable, natural parts of living.
Everything that receives the gift of life as we know it
Dies sometime, perhaps just moving on
To another part of life's journey
That we can't know or understand here and now.
But everything that lives dies eventually.
Life and death are one, inseparable.
Birth and death are both gifts from God,
And there are blessings in both events
And at every split second in between.
Even the hardships are blessings in some way,
As I see it.
Furthermore, God is present and loving
In each one of those split seconds.
God is in and around each event.
Romans 8 tells us
Nothing can separate us from the love of God.
I believe this.
Whether this particular moment/situation
Is rough or smooth,
God is always with us, loving us, holding us.
Even when we hurt, when we lose,
Even when we're cold or sick or scared.

Death comes fast to some people.
They drop in their tracks in the midst of a normal routine.
To some of us death comes slowly, in increments,
Some of which may be related to illness.
To me, these tangible evidences of our limited time
And resources are precious gifts.
They help us not to waste time
Or opportunities to love and live fully.
It is anything but easy to die slowly,
But I thank God for the insights it brings.
My illness has given me some of
My greatest and deepest blessings.

Deep and High Blessings

December 8, 1991
4:40 am

What are these "deep and high blessings"
I keep spouting off about?
Is this phrase just a clever cliché
I've dreamed up
To saccharinely apply
To get myself by,
Or to impress people?

I hope you don't for one second
Think that.

Deep and high blessings
Are the harder blessings!
They are not the standard ones
Like health,
Happiness, prosperity,
Good looks,
Or the Cubs beating the Cardinals.

Deep and high blessings often come
Through the sweat of the brow,
Through pain, loneliness,
And unfulfilled dreams.
They go in the direction their name implies:
Vertically.
Line drives and BMWs go horizontally.
Deep and high blessings,
In combination with our time line,
Make a cross.

Deep and high blessings
Are events I see which echo
What Jesus went through and exemplified.
Born of difficulty,
Requiring simplicity and integrity,
Independent of and transcending
Life's "ups and downs,"
Of eternal meaning;
Bringing profound,
And ultimately eternal,
Peace.

To David

December 8, 1991
5:00 am

Do you remember when you asked me
In the kitchen in Batavia
(Probably you were eleven),
"Mom, would you love me
If I grew sideburns like Elvis?"
I answered, "Yes, I would," with a smile.
"Mom," you continued,
"Would you love me
If I grew a mustache and beard?"
(This was in the seventies,
When hair like that had social significance!)
"I sure would, Sweetie!"
"Would you love me
If I let my beard grow
Down to my *bellybutton*?"
"Yup." Big smile.
"I'll love you always, no matter what."
You grinned then, and ran out to play.

Now you're twenty-five,
You're married
To a wonderful young woman, a theater star.
You're hobnobbing with the mayor of Indianapolis,
You regularly appear on TV and radio.
This week you're in DC
Collecting national awards
For your environmental work.
I'm intensely proud of you,
As I have been your whole life.

I've given you my disease,
And the anguish I feel about this
Is impossible for me to convey to you.
I, you, and now Michael share
This awful reality,
This threat.
All I can say now
Is what I told you
When you were eleven,
But through my tears this time.
I'll love you always, no matter what.

To Cami

December 8, 1991
5:15 am

Whoever gave us the impression life is easy?
Let's blame those old movies,
Like that one
Where Fred Astaire and Ginger Rogers
Danced on the ceiling.
Films from my early childhood, like
Miracle on Thirty-fourth Street
And Snow White,
Added to something about my personality,
Lulled me into thinking
Life was going to somehow be fine.

Now we know better don't we, dear?
"Life is difficult"
Hardly covers it, right?

But in the midst of the complications and heartaches,
You have grown, deepened, and are emerging
As a most wonderful person.
You are remarkably psychologically insightful,
Caring, thoughtful,
Supportive of me about
My career, my health,
And life in general.
You are intelligent, articulate, talented—
Oh! your pen and ink portraits!—
Interested and interesting
(Music, Egyptology, art history,
Film, theater set design, and more!)

Now you are pursuing a drafting career,
Getting good grades, working diligently.

I'm proud of you.
I treasure you as a daughter, friend, and human being.
Go for it!
You have so much potential!
And always remember
I'll love you *forever*,
No matter what.

Detach With Love

December 21, 1991
DK's—Evanston

One thing which is difficult for me to do is
Detach with love.
When I see things I feel are
Lacking or wrong,
Especially in the lives of my children,
I want to rush in,
Change, "fix."
It is hard to think
I may have very little real information,
Or my perception may be off.
It is not my business!
They are grown up.
To define my role as loving parent
Is tricky, complicated.

Surely sometimes God uses
My intelligence, concern,
Knowledge, love,
My integrity or courage
To reach people,
Especially my children,
Meaningfully.

Our minister, bless his heart, says,
"Nobody gets it exactly right, you know—
Cheer up! Stay with it."
As a human being, he says,
He deals with life's complexities
And goes ahead, many times,
When he is only 60 percent sure.
That is courageous, thoughtful,
Realistic, I feel.
That is how, albeit shakily, I will
Detach with love.

Everyone Has An Empty Place Inside

December 21, 1991
DK's—Evanston

They used to say
In my Bible study group back in the Midwest,
"Everyone has an empty place inside,
And it's in the shape of God."

Some people try to satisfy
That empty feeling
With food,
But no amount of food is enough,
Because the stomach is not the place
That needs to be filled.

Some people try to fill the void
With alcoholic drinks.
Alcohol deadens the feelings of emptiness,
So alcohol fools you into thinking
It has taken care of the problem.
But when the deadening effect wears off,
You feel the emptiness more
Than before you took your last drinks.
You feel even more empty.
You feel worse.

Some people try to fill the God-shaped place
With drugs, material possessions,
Non-stop activity, or sexual encounters, but
These don't fill the bill either.

When we realize it is a spiritual void we're feeling,
We have turned a corner.
Recognizing the reality of
Our spiritual life,
Our spiritual need,
Leads us in remarkable
New directions.

The Older I Get, the Less I Understand

December 21, 1991
DK's—Evanston

The older I get, the less I understand about life.
When I was young,
I saw everything clearly, and
I figured out life's answers quickly,
Right after the questions popped up.
As a matter of fact,
My list of answers
Ran well ahead of
The questions.
The answers list was lovely and long;
The questions list was relatively short,
And certainly manageable
In those days.

But the older I've become,
The more these lists have shifted.
Life has had time to intervene.
Now the questions
Far outnumber the solutions.
As a matter of fact,
Certainties are fast disappearing.
Black and white,
And with them, youthful bravado,
Have gradually become
A vast panoply of shades of gray.
Quiet thoughtfulness and prayerfulness
Have replaced
My earlier brash assuredness.
Oh yes, I've always prayed a lot, but
I used to pray, more often,
In cases of relative emergency.
When nothing I was doing seemed to be working,
I called God in.

There has been a gradual shift, until
Now I pray spontaneously
Throughout the day,
Wherever I am
For whatever is on my mind,
Or in my heart.

It seems to me now that
I understand very little
In the scheme of things.
I pray about almost everything.

I have come to see
My lack of knowledge
As a blessing.
God is now
My constant companion.

Today I Met Gene Montgomery

December 21, 1991
DK's—Evanston

Today I met Gene Montgomery.
He is in his eighty-seventh year,
Tall, bearded, distinguished,
A painter of wonderful portraits.
His home is small, charming,
And filled with his work.
"It pays to advertise," he chuckled.
He led us up to his attic studio.
It was neat and lovely,
With a large north cathedral window
Displaying on its upper sill
A collection of glass bottles of many colors.
On the easel was
The latest masterful corporate portrait.
Sitting on the floor was
A wild self-portrait,
Done more than fifty years ago,
Of this ferocious young painter
Looking back over his shoulder at us
With an amazingly virile scowl.
He is like my father now,
A gentleman, soft-spoken,
Intelligent, gracious.
He shared a story about modeling
For an Abraham Lincoln sculpture
By Laredo Taft in the late 1930s.

I was inspired and warmed
By my encounter with Mr. Montgomery.
"I want to be like you when I grow up," I laughed.
But inside I was crying a little,
Wondering, How much time?
To see, to be well, to paint...
How long do I dare to hope I have?

MRI in NYC 12/31/91
to Mayo Clinic 1/6/92
brain surgery 1/8/92

We Are Each on Our Path to the Infinite

December 21, 1991
DK's—Evanston

We are each on our path to the infinite.
From the moment of our conception,
Perhaps infinitely before that,
We wend our one-of-a-kind way
Toward the ineffable.
Each person,
Each path,
Each moment
Is sacred beyond our comprehension.
There are as many paths as there are persons;
All are of ultimate value
In their unending variety.

This is why we must take special care
Not to try to coerce anyone
To do it "my way."
We can accompany each other sometimes
For a while,
We can embrace one another
As our paths cross,
Hail and encourage each other
During our convergings and pauses.

But "my way" is only,
In the final analysis,
For me.
Every other person's "way" is only
For him or for her.
The choices,
The directions are,
Whether or not we know or remember it,
Between the individual and God:
Countless holinesses.

Please

January 6, 1992
4:30 pm
Mayo Clinic West 1
Preadmissions

Please
Don't come around here
Looking smug
Because you're more well
Right now
Than I am.

Please
Don't say things like,
"If you had only gone on a
Strictly vegetarian diet
Years ago (like I did),
This wouldn't have happened."
"If you had only been
More positive..."
"If you had only prayed right..."
(According to whom?)
"If only you had accepted Jesus
As your personal Saviour..."
(I did, a long, long time ago.)

Please
Don't make me feel worse.
Don't blame me for being ill.
Don't shame me
For my genetic defect.

Please.

Thank You

January 7, 1992
St. Mary's Hospital
Before the angiogram

Thank you,
Drs. von Hippel and Lindau.
You have given me
The concrete guideposts
To a marvelously full life.

Some people have called me
"Hyper."
But I have only been hurrying
So that I could enjoy
And participate in
As much of life as possible.
Since age nineteen,
An insistent inner voice
Has kept telling me
My life might be abbreviated.
So I have worked hard,
Played and prayed hard,
I have run fast, yes,
Have had a wild schedule
Sometimes.
But sometimes
I have lain very still
For very long periods.

Some people have called me
"Intense" and "intentional."
But I have only been trying
To make meaning,
Take in the meaning of life.
When there is a small space
Or a limited time factor
Things get a bit crowded,
Condensed.
People who have more time,
Who feel less pressured,
Naturally cannot relate.
They resist, even get hostile
Sometimes.

But heavenly things have been accomplished!
Mending and washings
Of dishes, clothes, and cars,
Mundane "little things"
That weave the fabric
Of a sunny, peaceful life.

Love-making and pregnancies,
Blessed mystery of gestation and births.
Infinite preciousness
Of infants, toddlers,
Children growing.
Lunches with the kids
In the Morton Arboretum,
Then lying on the blanket,
Watching the clouds
Through the branches of
The amazing variety of trees.
Church school teaching,
A weekly meeting of twelve Cub Scouts
In the basement.
Batavia Little League and Girls' Softball games,
Sometimes in three parks
Simultaneously!
Talking on the phone
While baking a cake
And making dinner
And helping with homework.
A dining room table holding
Oil paints and portrait-in-progress,
Sewing materials
For eight Christmas aprons,
And a stack of presents and wrappings
Two feet high.
There was the year's work
With the kids at the John F. Kennedy Center
In Aurora,
Field trips with the handicapped
Teens at Batavia High,
All of the wonders of
Five years of Vietnamese resettlement,
And in New York,
Friday afternoons at
Booker T. Washington Learning Center,
Hospitality for the Homeless

At All Souls Church,
And at Advent Lutheran,
The Saturday soup kitchen.
I have loved every minute of it,
Hectic as it has been.
I thrive on activity.
I relish challenge.
It is all so precious,
So holy.

Some people have called me
"Weird."
I went out and marvelled
At the fuzziness of new soybeans
In the spring fields.
I took my children,
And later my best friend,
To share my awe
At how the corn stalks grow upwards
In ever-opening spirals:
One of the countless examples
All around us
All the time
Of ultimate order—
God's handiwork,
God's incredible, irresistible
Artistic design,
Always ours for the taking in.
My joy was unbounded
In those fields.
I hugged trees too,
And I'm so very glad
I did.
Again,
Precious, holy.
My viewpoint hasn't changed one iota.
This level of appreciation,
To me,
Is weird
Like ecstasy is weird.
I wish everyone
This weirdness.

Some people have found it
Amusing, confusing,

Some very tiring, even exasperating,
How so much,
So many people especially
Could be so beautiful,
So dear to me.
I have never seen a person
In whom there is no beauty.
And I am always looking!
The unending variety of people
In New York City
Delights and fascinates me.
Whether on the streets
Or the subways,
The potpourri of faces makes me feel
Like a kid in a candy shop.
Loveliness everywhere!

And so I have had
This wonder-filled
Love affair with Life
All of these years.
Where will it lead next?
Wherever it is,
I will surely find
Beautiful things there.

Thank you,
Drs. von Hippel and Lindau.
Thank you, Lord.

Patty

January 7, 1992
St. Mary's 3:00 pm
Before the angiogram
Prior to brain surgery

Last night I took the bus
To Apache Mall,
Rochester, Minnesota.
There were only three of us
Riding.

A young woman sat across from me,
Staring, lips apart.
Our eyes met.
"What's your name?" she asked loudly.
"Karen," I replied.
"What's yours?"
"I'm Patty," she answered.
She talked to the driver
In a childlike voice.
Her perhaps thirty years
Were not evident
In her behavior or speech.
But she radiated a goodness,
A sweetness.
I liked her.

While I waited for the nine o'clock bus
To take me back to town and my hotel,
Patty was there with me.
She came up with
Straightforward directness,
Said hi,
And struck up
A remarkable,
Moving,
Conversation.
Looking at me intensely, curiously,
She asked with great seriousness,
"Have you been in a accident?"
"You mean my left eye?" I queried.
"Yes."
"No, it's just very sick.

It has been blind for many years," I said.
"Ohhh, that's too bad," she answered,
With great empathy.
"I am very fort'nate,
Because God has given me a handicap.
I'm a very special person."

A tear welled up in my sad left eye.
(The right one is totally dry now.)
She told me
About living at the state hospital,
About the group home where
"A nasty person
Wanted to suck my breasts,"
And about her lovely
Rochester foster parents
Of the last two years.
She takes the bus
To Apache Mall
Almost every night
For a "little treat."

Ah, Patty!
You, with your story,
Were my evening's only companion,
My precious gift from God
On this marker night of my life.

Brain surgery
Mayo Clinic
January 8, 1992

Sacred Process

March 10, 1992
Radiation day four

There is something
Inside me
More substantial than
A kidney or an ovary.
Something which cannot be
Cut away or altered or
Overcome.

There is something linked
Not just to flesh and blood,
Though that now is so,
But connected also somehow
To eternity.
Something that will not always need
Oxygen or light,
Water or food.
Every time another part of me
Is removed or invaded,
This eternity-linked part
Shows itself to me
A little more surely,
A little more clearly.

It is all part of
The sacred process
Of my life.
All is well
Peace
All is well.

Every Day

March 12, 1992
Memorial Sloan-Kettering Hospital

Many times I've jokingly said,
"Everyday life takes up every day!"
Maybe it's my way of excusing
Disorganization or procrastination:
No time to draw or paint
I'm too busy
With mundane things.

Now I'm at a juncture in my life
Where radiation treatments
And health-related activities—
Yes, bill-paying and insurance—
Seem to take up all my energy and focus.
By the time I get ready to go
I'm tired,
Every day.
I rest and sleep all morning.
I guess it's depression
As much as anything.

Today I'll pick up my wigs.
Every day I pick up miso soup to drink.
My health-conscious friends say
Miso helps fight radiation's side effects.
I also drink carrot juice (for beta-carotene)
From my new juicer
Every day.

Each telephone call,
And much of the non-business mail,
Focuses on my illness.
Isn't that enough to
Make anyone tired?
My identity has changed:
Others see me as sick.
How can I not begin to think of myself
That way?

Next week I'll get my hair cut
Very short.
For years, in my

Everyday frustration with my long hair,
I have threatened, kiddingly,
To get a crew cut.
Next week it will happen.
It may ease my horror
As all my hair falls out.

I am trying
To meditate, concentrate on goodness,
To believe that God is present in this process
Every day.
I pray on that radiation table,
Pray for personal peace,
And for everyone connected
To these events.

Surely there will be
An everyday existence
After all of this,
Won't there?

Twins

March 22, 1992
Sunday, 5:00 pm
Day after the haircut

For several years
In the early to mid-eighties
I dreamed repeatedly, regularly, about
Twins.
Sometimes I would be pregnant with twins.
Once I dreamed
Of giving birth to twins.
Sometimes they would be young children;
One time they were about eleven.
All of the dreams were lovely,
Comforting, happy.

I was in therapy then.
My psychologist and I
Would wonder together,
Would muse,
Who are these twins?
Of course we could never
Come up with a definitive answer.
But the moments he and I spent,
And the hours I spent inwardly
Thinking, pondering,
Trying to solve this lovely puzzle
Were sweet, very pleasurable.

When the love of my life
Came into my life
The dream period and his appearance,
Even at a great geographical distance,
Overlapped.
As our relationship
Began to take form,
It came to light
He was a twin.
I wondered privately,
Could these two men
Have anything to do with
My lovely dreams?

As time went on,
As my waking dreams
Were quickened and nourished,
Fred (my psychologist)
And I smilingly, bemusedly,
In increasing wonder,
Began to believe
My dear love
And his dear brother
Might well be they
Of my comfort—
My twin joys.
In time my love and I were wed.
I never knew life could be so wonderful.

Today, after a six-day, delightful visit,
My brother-in-law
Flew back to Chicago.
As my husband and I are
Soul mates,
My brother-in-law is a kindred spirit.
I connect with each of them
So amazingly!
Each of them is such a joy to me.
I know now that they are indeed
My long-heralded
Twins.

The way I see it,
God sent these two to me.
But before they physically arrived
In my life,
He gently and so deftly
Prepared me
For their arrival.
As they came closer,
It was as though He were planning
The most beautiful party for me—
A birthday—no, birth*ing* party.
For my life was to begin
Anew.
He gave me new hints,
Dropped luscious, delightful clues
And let me ponder, figure, puzzle
Over them with

Increasing excitement and pleasure.
It was a marvelous
Gestation, you see—
A quickening—
Yes, a new life
For me beginning.

Now they are fully in my life,
These twins.
Though in many ways
Life has never been
More transitory,
More harrowing, than now,
Yet with these twins in it,
Life has never been
More spectacular,
More comforting or comfortable for me.
I never dreamed
Life could be so wonderful.
—Oh, but perhaps I did!

I am profoundly joyous,
Profoundly grateful.
Thank you, thank you, Lord!

Lilly Lives On

March 23, 1992

Whither thou goest I will go.
Wherever thou lodgest I will lodge.
Thy people shall be my people...
RUTH 1:15

My first pastel still life
Was of a beautiful fluted silver basket,
Filled with Macintosh apples.
The basket shimmers and shines,
Reflecting the apples' red and green hues
With every turn, every etched detail.
Basket and fruit glow
Against a dark background.

I call the painting
"Lilly's Basket, Bearing Fruit."
The basket belonged to my mother-in-law.
I think of her very often,
Even now,
Years after her death.
She was so accepting of me,
And we had such a love
For one another.
Through this painting she,
With her gentle, quiet demeanor,
Lives on.

Lilly also lives on
Through the fruit of her womb,
Her twin sons,
One of whom is my husband.
They too are kind and gentle,
Loving, accepting,
Intelligent, insightful.
Yes, they are gentle men
In the most literal and lovely sense.
They nurture me as no other has.
My life, with them in it, becomes
More amazing,
More wonder-full,
More fun!
As time goes along.

Again I am moved to prayer:
I thank you, Lord, that
Lilly lives on.

Being With You Is Like Being With Myself

March 25, 1992
Steven and David's
48th birthday

It seems impossible to me,
But I've found two people
With whom I'm so comfortable,
So relaxed,
That I can just be myself,
And so can they.
This is new stuff for me.
I have found something like it
With a few women friends,
And earlier in my life with my parents
And my children,
But this is beyond my expectations!

How could it be
That we have found this peace,
This fun, this meeting
Of minds and hearts?
Gentile woman and twin Jewish men,
They from tiny Catlin, Illinois,
One a doctor, the other a poet and English professor,
Each dignified and precious;
I, a blond Swede from East Rockford,
An artist, writer, searcher…

I cannot know how all this has come about.
I just thank God and marvel
At what I cannot—need not—know.
And for you, dear Steven and David,
I have the ultimate compliment:
Being with you is like being with myself.
Aren't we the luckiest?

Fried chicken
birthday dinner
followed!

To Michael

March 27, 1992

Beautiful, doe-eyed boy
Middle child
You often sat quietly,
Looking pensive,
As a baby.
Quiet, beautiful—
My "breather child"—
Between two
More vociferous, rambunctious
Than you.

As you grew
I remember you,
Waking and sleeping,
Running, playing in the usual ways,
But also
Playing with language.
Friskie, our funny dog
Became "Fo-Kosk-Keedle-Euk."
A merry laugh accompanied.
I loved you so.

You've always been
Sensitive, a little shy,
Gentle,
Wishing to do no harm;
Rather to help, to encourage,
To nurture people,
To build up,
Never to tear down.

And what a worker!
Paper route at the
Batavia apartments—
Remember how
We'd get up at five o'clock
Sunday mornings
And deliver huge heavy
Beacon Newses
To all of them?
Remember our more-than-interesting
Collection attempts there?

You baby-sat,
Did lawns,
Labored
As all-around
Down'n' dirty helper
At the Cadillac garage.
Then there were summer jobs
Digging ditches and
Doing maintenance
For the gas company.

Now you are a college grad.
Salesman by day,
Breaking your own records regularly.
And by night
You moonlight
So your dear wife, Beth, can stay at home,
Taking the homemaker/mother role.
That was my role, too.
Could it be that your choices now
Are in some way a reflection
Of your positive feelings
About how I did things
As you were growing up?
I hope so.

I always wish you the very best:
Deepest and highest blessings.
My heart goes with you
Always and ever,
Dear son.

More Bad News

April 20, 1992
After hearing Michael's diagnosis

Oh no...oh no...oh no...
Oh no...no...no...
Why? Why? Why?
I can't stand it
I can't take it
I can't take anymore!
It's too much
It's just too, too much...
I feel like the California man,
Rodney King,
Lying on the pavement
In fetal position
Now curled up
With arms over my head and face
Being beaten, kicked
Repeatedly, unmercifully,
By the powers that be.
I feel bombed,
With nothing left but
Charred uprights,
Small fires, smoke,
In desolation.
How can my heart break again,
Now for my second child,
And ever mend again?
How can I go on?

Companion piece:
It's Okay Today
May 20, 1992

I'm Still Here!

April 24, 1992

(Adapted to the tune of "Jimmy Cracked Corn;"
to be sung with fun and clapping)

My kidney is gone,
But I'm still here.
My ovaries too,
But I'm still here.
My omentum is out,
My hearing is down,
My left eye is blind,
But I'm still around. } Refrain melody

I've been surgically cut
And the wolf's been at the door
More times than I can count,
I suspect there will be more.
It seems as though the rests
That I've had in between
Aren't coming anymore.
It's a real battle scene. } Refrain melody

Yes, there'll be more cuts and sutures,
Radiation—it's not easy,
And laser, I suppose.
It's enough to make me queasy!
But when they've done it all
And my sun sinks in the west,
Hope the message you remember
Is the one I love the best: } Refrain melody

I may not be in sight,
But everything's all right
Love and Spirit keep me with you.
I'm still here! } Refrain melody, slowly

Have You Ever Really Looked at a Tulip?

April 25, 1992

Have you ever really looked at a tulip?
Six amazingly cool, smooth, scalloped petals
Open very slowly, over days,
To show us the geometric perfection
Inside.
The one I'm looking at
Is purest yellow.
In the center of the flower's floor is a design
Of deepest indigo blue.
Two dark compositions,
Like two exquisite sets of brush strokes,
Appear on alternate petal bases
To make a nearly black backdrop
For the six-segmented stamen,
Lumpy with heavy pollen load,
And plump green pistil,
At the tip of which glows
The brilliant yellow, three-armed stigma.
Looking at it straight on,
Against its indigo background,
I imagine a jubilant bird
Riding the air currents.

The tulip:
Another example of God's perfect order.
The beauty of the tangible
Points to
The incalculable bounty,
The mystery of the ineffable.
My heart cannot contain
My awe,
My joy.

(Pastel painting followed)

And Yet...

May 11, 1992

Does it mean something, then,
That I've lived,
And live still?
What has my life added up to?
Short on college degrees
No "job," no salary
No fame or fortune
No prestige
No worldly power
And yet...
My daughter and daughters-in-law
Love, support, and praise me.
My sons are loving and caring,
Concerned for my safety
And well-being.
Son David writes poetry
To and for me,
As does my wonderful brother-in-law David,
And my dear friend Carolyn.
My husband has written me
Profound, sweetest thoughts
In his letters,
Which echo and augment
His tender concern, love and devotion
Every day.

There is a steady stream
Of support from parents, sister,
Family and friends.

Past battles continue.
The present is fraught with difficulties.
The future is so uncertain,
Looks so ominous, frightening,
And yet...
Goodness, preciousness
Surround me.
My life has great meaning.
All will, somehow, be well.

Brought back from the edge
of despair by son David's poem,
Always, and his wife Shannon's
incredible letter at Mother's Day.

About Time

May 17, 1992
12:25 am

God has all of eternity
Within which to work,
It's true.
But that doesn't let us off the hook.

It is our sacred responsibility
To work diligently with Him/Her,
Doing all we can
To use our precious gift of time
Well.

God needs us all to be partners,
Thoughtful, prayerful,
Active and eager
To make the world as good a place
As it can be.

It's Okay Today

May 20, 1992

These last months have brought
One blow after another.
One more frightening fact to incorporate
One more lump to live with
One more examination
One more consultation
One more threat to sight
One more angiogram
One more laser
One more symptom
One more MRI
One more surgery
Mine
My children's
My mother's and father's
My friends'
One, and then one more
Source of worry, anxiety, fear.
How to go on?

Let us pray to learn,
Through some miracle,
To live *now,*
With focus on what is left,
And then to enjoy, use, savor these things.
Let us not waste time cowering before
The next imagined difficulty.
Life is still manageable!
It is possible to celebrate life as it is.
It is possible to work, play, *live*.

Even as reduced as we are,
Today is all any of us has.
It is different from yesterday,
And will change again tomorrow,
But it's okay today.
Let us focus on the positives and
Build upon them now.
Let us let go of the fears
That we have been clutching about us
Like enveloping blankets.

Let them fall away.
Let us dare to get up
And refresh ourselves.
Even with all that has happened
Let us dress, venture out, and
Be part of the world again.
Let's go for it!
It's okay today.

Written in response to my poem
More Bad News
April 20, 1992

I Fight

July 10, 1992
1:30 am

Everyone thinks of me as
Timid, quiet, patient, passive,
Certainly more of a lover than a fighter.
But I fight, every day.

I fight depression,
Observing my slow but definite decline
At the whims of
von Hippel-Lindau disease
And the cancer that has followed.
No matter how I try
To live in and appreciate
Each day,
I fight discouragement and depression.

I fight anger, indeed rage at times
That not only has this disease
Blighted my life,
But the lives of both my sons, their wives,
And yes, by association, my daughter.
And now my precious newborn grandson
Is threatened.
It hurts, worries, and angers me
More than words can express.

I fight feelings of frustration
And aggravation about principles.
I am female in a sexist world.
I have very little personal power
As the world measures.
No titles follow my name.
There has been little money of my own making.

My art career was cut off prematurely
By my illness.

The spiritual values and life styles
To which I have committed
Have often seemed not to be shared
By significant others near me.
As a matter of fact,
Not only have I felt

Unappreciated, unaffirmed
To a great extent—
It is clear at times that
I am still considered a fool, a patsy,
A sucker by some
To whom I extend myself.
I am taken advantage of,
Ignored, even scorned.

I now try to remember
The Biblical admonition
Not to cast my pearls before the swine;
If certain people reject me
Or my heartfelt truths/ideas/ideals,
It is okay, after a reasonable amount
Of time, effort, and energy
Have been expended,
To simply
"Shake the dust off my sandals
And move on."
But how, and where,
In my present condition?

I fight lethargy and fatigue,
Mostly because of the physical toll
Of my illness.
But fatigue is complicated by
Isolation.
Oh, for a "regular job,"
With its daily structure,
Companionship of others,
Motivation and stimulation.
No matter how mundane one's achievements,
They bring certain satisfactions.

I fight fear:
Fear of losing my remaining vision,
Fear of more cancer spread,
Fear of losing the patience and caring
Of those around me
As my strength diminishes,
Fear for my children's
And grandchildren's future,
Both medically and financially.

I pray a lot, too.
I try to stay interested and active
Today.
I try to stay in a
Grateful, positive, "normal" mode.
"Who has it easy?" I ask myself.
"Keep at it! Life is precious."
Some days this strategy works better than others.

So! you see,
This sweet, affable person
Is at war with many things—
Too many to mention here.
I'm a fighter.
But this fighter
Is getting very tired.

Paradox

July 10, 1992
2:00 am

Even as two cells become four,
Four eight,
We are on our journey
Not just developing a life,
But slipping toward death.
No, wait, don't protest.
Don't turn away.
It's okay.

No two snowflakes are identical,
And yet all are snow.
Each person is absolutely unique,
Even if he is an "identical" twin.
We struggle to be strong,
To be independent, in control,
And yet it seems to me now
We perhaps have the most potential
For growth, for deepening as persons
When that coveted control slips,
When we are weakened somehow
And our dependence,
In spite of all we can humanly do,
Is painfully obvious.

As I age,
In addition to
Real insights I feel I have gained,
I see and feel acutely
What I *cannot* know.
The more my years
And life experiences,
The more real becomes my quandary
At explaining life—
Any big or little part of it.
I have now reached the point
Where I honestly believe,
And often say,
Everything is mystery.

It seems that this concept
Should make life more insecure,
More frightening than ever.
The paradox is, somehow
It makes things more bearable.
The picture is
So big,
So complex, and
I am so small and relatively powerless,
My anxiety shrinks
To insignificant
In the scheme of it all.

Earthly demise and death
Are difficult, yes,
But just, I believe, another stage
Of life.
I dread parts of the journey toward death,
But look forward to death
At the same time.
Sacred process is wrapped
In
Paradox.

Gift

September 18, 1992

My life is God's gift to me.
What I do with my life
And the way I die
Are my gifts to Him.
I, in my flawed way,
Have tried to dedicate my life
To the divine, the sacred,
Living as fully and gratefully
As I could.
Life has been amazing,
Wonderful and awesome
Even at the hardest times.
At death, it will be
My privilege, my dearest wish,
To give this life
To the eternal One,
The source of life.
To me, God is real.
God is love, goodness, and light.
God is eternal.
But perhaps most wonderful
Is the knowledge that
We are joined with Him, even now,
Inextricably,
Even in our human imperfection.
Yes! Now *and* forever.
Hallelujah!

It Comes to Me

October 6, 1992
After our family reunion in Indianapolis

Most days I keep my sadness
Below the surface,
Denying my feelings of
Fear, grief,
And go, as best I can,
About my life
As though
Everything is normal, okay.
But once in a while
It comes to me.
It engulfs me,
Washes over and under me,
And I get carried away,
Dissolving in tears.
My grief can be triggered by
An event, or
No event.
I become gradually unable
To contain my emotions.
I know it's good
To feel these feelings,
To let them out
Occasionally.
When it's over, I feel
Not just relieved,
But somehow
Satisfied,
In some way renewed,
Able once again somehow
To go on.
Feelings of quietude
And personal peace
Follow.

How Are You Today? How Do You Feel?

October 23, 1992

Everyone's concern comes out immediately:
"How are you today?"
"How do you feel?"
I have clever, joking
Stock answers,
To be used as I pass,
And accompanied by a hearty laugh.
"You can't keep a mean,
One-eyed Midwestern woman down," I grin.
People are relieved at my levity.
Most don't pursue it,
Simply return my wave and big smile.
Or I reply cheerfully,
"Hanging in there!"
If I know the questioner better
I get closer to the truth,
But it causes a feeling of
Vulnerability and
A level of intimacy
That often makes me quite uncomfortable.
I tell almost no one
How I often really feel:
Frightened, first and foremost.
Filled with dread.
Profoundly sad.
I have often said,
"I don't mind dying—
It's what I have to go through
In the meantime."
It's almost impossible to avoid
Visions of what may come.
It's very difficult
To keep a clear mind
For the unfettered living
To be done here and now;
To remember
I'm really quite well today!

Good Memories Sustain

October 23, 1992
12:15 pm

I think of all the things
That felt so good when I was little:
Dad gently rubbing my feet,
So relaxing me as to put me to sleep;
My mother's cool hand
Resting on my feverish forehead;
Her fresh chocolate cake,
Still warm from the oven,
My heavenly after-school snack.
My dad's delightfully silly
"Sack of potatoes,
Rotten tomatoes" song.
How he and I laughed, loved,
And enjoyed each other!
Bubble baths and stories before bed,
Working with Dad in the victory garden.
My grandma's
Hearty laugh,
Wonderful homemade breads,
Pasties* and soups,
Her cheery, "How lovely you *look!*"
Our long canasta games
(Sometimes she'd let me win);
And wonderful Sunday dinners.
Aunt Ethel's dear giggles
And sweet gentle ways.
Her company's beautiful
Yards of woolen fabrics and linings,
The remnants of which my mother used
To make my lovely winter coats.
Taking care of my infant sister,
Talking baby talk to her
And delighting in her strong kicks
And wonderful smiles.
All these, and countless more
Good memories
Sustain me.

*Pasties (pass´tees) are a traditional food—a meat, potato and vegetable pie from the British Isles; my mother's family originated in Cornwall, England.

Thoughts of Heaven

October 25, 1992
Sunday, 3:30 pm

When my life here is finished,
I will gladly give it over
To the Divine One,
And His/Her continuing process.
I will go to meet the Creator
In a new and different place:
A place more complete, more joyful,
More comforting
Than anything
I have thus far known or imagined.

Treadmill

October 26, 1992
Before visit to throat surgeon
to discuss another needle biopsy

I feel like
I'm on a treadmill
Which is set
To increase speed,
Incrementally but automatically.
There is no way for me
To stop the machine
And no way for me to get off it.
Rest is impossible;
All I can do is try to keep up.
I get more and more fatigued
As time goes on,
Feeling a little more
Helpless
Frustrated
Now becoming
Really frightened,
Coming up on desperate.
How can I go on?

I can't understand this process.
I have great difficulty
Being patient with myself.
How then will those around me
Understand or be patient with me?
It is already difficult
For my husband to slow his pace,
Waiting for slow me all the time.
I love him so and
Want so badly for him
To be happy with me.
I must keep striving
For normalcy.

It's terrifying
Getting used to the idea
That I am losing the battle
For my health and life.
I can't accept it yet.

Must keep fighting
To keep even.
Reach down for more strength.
I can't give up.

Someone said recently,
"Look, everything is going to be all right.
Each of us lives until we die.
Just let go;
Surrender
To the process."
That day will come, of course.
But not today.
Not now, not yet.
Please?

Treadmill II

November 1, 1992
Awaiting needle biopsy report

It seems life has become
A treadmill
Which, no matter what I do,
Or how I feel,
Incrementally only goes faster.
Illness adds to natural aging
To slow me down.
The treadmill has
No "off" button.
It keeps speeding up,
Gradually but
Relentlessly.
I'm so tired
I really feel unequal to the task
A fair amount of the time.
It's just a matter of
When I finally
Will have to
Give in.

Noting a Significant Change

November 5, 1992
After receiving needle
biopsy report indicating
the presence of another
metastasis

Another batch of bad news
Came our way yesterday.
But, strangely,
With this latest threat
To my life
I did not shed a tear.
I remained amazingly
Calm and matter of fact.
I guess we could
Just chalk up this behavior as
A straightforward response
To another in a long series of crises;
Maybe they aren't
Going to affect me
To the same degree anymore.
Or is it that simple?
At this point
I feel strangely removed,
Distanced, it seems,
From my own situation,
My own story.
Am I taking my first steps
Into the late stage
Of the grief process,
Acceptance?
Or is the "composure" I feel
Depression in masquerade?

Poetry is Born of Pain

November 15, 1992
After David and Joyce's visit

Sometimes I think
My poetry well
Has run dry.
Several weeks (months) go by;
No poems come.
Then something happens
Which moves me,
Prods me,
Brings my awareness back
To my real-life drama,
And—
Lo and behold!
The poems flow again.
Memories are stirred,
My heart is touched.
My emotions come to the surface.
I am taken
And shaken
Again.
My poetry,
Very often,
Is born of pain.

Mixed Bag

December 13, 1992
On the Metroliner to Baltimore

Thinking of how many
Material things
We accumulate,
Either by necessity
Or striving,
It came to me that

Our belongings,
Even if they begin
As our fond desires,
Every one,
At some point,
Becomes a burden.

Most Precious Parcel

December 13, 1992
3:00 pm
On the Metroliner to Baltimore

A very light little package
Arrived one recent day.
I greeted it with intense curiosity.
What could this be?
It was damaged and
Hanging partially open.
Had its contents spilled from it?

When I got it open,
I burst into tears.
It contained some of my most beloved objects:
A number of fall leaves
Of all sizes, shapes, and colors;
An ear of field corn,
Rock-hard and hardy;
And a handful of
Beautiful little
Acorns!

These, sent by my son and his wife,
Please me more than money
Or jewels or furs.
Their hearts and my heart met
In that
Most precious parcel.

After forty-odd years
Spent among the flora and fauna
Of Illinois,
Surrounded all of that time
By fields of
Corn, wheat, oats, and soybeans,
I have a special feeling
For simple and common
Natural objects.
Seven years of living in New York City
Have intensified my feelings:
The lowly field corn, acorns, and
The leaves are, every one,
A miracle.

The simplest things
Are often the most splendid things.
It is as if,
By bringing these into being,
God sought to make
Her/His continuing creation
And love for us
Understandable to us.

Come, take time
To look
Thoughtfully, carefully
At nature
Both outdoors and inside,
Up close—
A magnifying glass helps!—
And be
Amazed
With me.

Small World

December 13, 1992
3:30 pm
On the Metroliner to Baltimore

As my illness progresses,
My world
Becomes progressively smaller.
One day I became
Exquisitely aware,
While sitting at my kitchen window,
Of the beauty
Of the cyclamen plant there.
It was a revelation.
I looked with
Wonder and amazement.
It spoke to my spirit,
Saying,
You are not alone,
Even for an instant.
God is gifting you
Intensely,
Though in different ways now,
Just as He/She always has.
My gratefulness
Borders on delirium sometimes.
I am so limited these days,
And yet at times
So deeply happy!

On the Train to Baltimore

December 13, 1992
4:00 pm
Facing possible blindness
in my only seeing eye

This morning
I wasn't at all sure
I could go through
With this trip.

Anticipating
More bad news
Seemed more than
I could stand.

My tear flood,
Released in the arms
Of my tender husband,
Would not stop.
Tears merged with
Shower water,
Then soaked
Into my towel
As I dried myself.

And then I could go on.
In eighteen hours
I'll begin to know
My new reality.

Trouble Spot

December 13, 1992
4:20 pm
On the Metroliner to Baltimore

Now that my last scare
Is at least somewhat resolved
I've noticed something else:
A new spot in my seeing eye.
It's right near
My center vision.
It is small,
But it is just below
The very center
Of my visual field.
When I read,
It obscures part
Of the line below my focus.

How terrifying to think
That now, after
My art has been
Taken from me,
Reading and writing
May also become impossible.
How could I endure?
How could life
Even approach
Manageability?
How could I not sink
Into utter despair?

And yet,
Even as I think
These thoughts,
Something in me says,
No—I could learn to cope.
I've been blind
Or nearly so for
A number of periods
Of my life;
I have somehow coped.
We will find ways.
Life will still be good.

Life will be different,
But there are discoveries
To be made at every juncture.
I already know from experience
Beauty spots endure,
Even in the presence of
Trouble spots.
It's not over yet!
Life will still be good.

Let's: A Light Verse

December 13, 1992
On the Metroliner to Baltimore
4:45 pm

Let's not live in the future,
(Too scary)
Let's not live in the past.
Let's live in
Right here, right now
Let's make this moment last.
Let us celebrate beauty
Right here where we are.
If we think
We'll never make it,
We may just have to
Fake it.
The important thing
Is the mind-set we bring;
Soon we'll find joy and take it!
Take it to heart,
Take it to soul,
In spite of all obstacles,
Growing more whole.
Perhaps we might even
Pass joy along—
In the midst of our heartaches,
We can still find a song.

Invitation

December 14, 1992

Dear God,
Surround me,
Touch me,
Enter me,
Fill me,
Saturate me
Until
You emanate from me,
Moving on to
Those around me.

Holy Spirit,
Come live in me.
Make me your crucible,
Your vessel,
One source of
Your limitless
Love and peace.

Amen.

Companion piece to
With Your Love and Peace, Lord

Long Minnesota Sunset

December 27, 1992
5:15 pm
Day after vomiting blood;
On way to Mayo Clinic—again

This majesty, splendor,
This grandeur,
This amazing show
Of rose and ochre,
Scarlet and deep purple
Assures me,
Everything will be okay.
No matter what happens,
God is with us,
Knows our story, and
Loves us.
Everything will be okay.

This incredible,
Seemingly endless panorama
Is the most awesome reminder:
Every moment is sacred
Everywhere.
No matter what
The diagnosis,
The prognosis,
Everything is,
And will continue to be,
Okay.

Turning Over a New Leaf

January 10, 1993

It seriously occurred to me yesterday
That my effort to keep going,
To "work through" deep fatigue,
Isn't working very well.
It is one thing to rest and sleep
When an acute situation
Is relentlessly, obviously
Holding you down.
It is harder though,
At least for me,
To want to continue
Extra sleep and rest
When my illness subsides
And is less dramatic,
Chronic.
Then I become impatient
For the old activity levels.
But as much as I try,
My fatigue erodes
My energy and effectiveness
Until I am robot-like,
Dismal, just wandering around
Aimlessly,
Accomplishing next to nothing.

Starting now,
I must lie down when
My body tells me to,
Sleeping until I wake,
At least part of the time.
I've been thinking
It is probably good
To "tough it out"
Hoping to fake my way
Through this,
And be the stronger for it.
But perhaps this
Deliberate going at cross-purposes
With my insistent body
Is even doing me harm.

Starting today,
I will listen better,
Rest more.
Maybe this new regimen
Will serve me better.
I hope and pray so.

Tender Benediction: A Dream

January 11, 1993
Morning, on waking

"The Lord bless you and keep you—"
Christian benediction
Is heard clearly,
Sweet note by sweet note
Sung by a perfectly balanced group
Of fine, moved and moving
Singers, a cappella.

I wake with a calm peace,
In the midst
Of a flowing
Of tender emotion.
I relate my dream to my husband.
I see him affected positively
By my telling of it.

What a marvelous way
To start a day!
Thank you,
Thank you,
Thank you, dear Lord.

Squabbling

January 19, 1993

"His steadfast love endures forever!" PSALM 106:1

If our
Different religions
Are separating us
From our fellow human beings,
Our God
Is too small.

Who created
Catholics, Lutherans, Baptists?
Who made Jews, Hindus, Muslims?
Who created humankind
In His own image?
Who has been present always,
And active in all of history?
Who is the alpha and omega,
The beginning and the end?
Is all of this for just a few?
Would a loving God,
Heavenly Father/Mother
Disown vast numbers of Her children,
After tenderly and with ultimate love
Bringing them into being?

The Underside of These Inspiring Poems

January 20, 1993

Fatigue
Fear
Sorrow
Shock
Anger
Confusion
Memory loss
Anxiety
Tension
Too little time
Too much time
Observing my own
Slow but certain demise.

Pain
Anguish
Sadness
Nausea, vomiting
Feeling vaguely different,
Not quite right, not quite well.
Adding steadily to my list
Of symptoms and trouble spots.

Gradually, incrementally
Giving up my identity
As a well person,
Then as a person
In and of the world.
Giving up being able
To effectively run my life.
Gradually trading
Wanting to participate for
Wanting to avoid participation
In the world outside.

Some days now
Everything seems
Like too much.
Too cold outside.
Too far to the store.
Too hard,

Too tiring,
Too long,
Too much...

All of these things
Swirl around in my head
Until it borders on mental chaos,
Insistently hounding my consciousness
Until I'm exhausted,
Reduced to nearly total inaction,
And must lie down
To sleep—
My only psychic rest.

Waking respites
Include my reading, meditation,
Poems and prayers;
These last two have become inseparable.

Parpie the Magnificent

January 31, 1993
10:00 pm
After holding and petting
Parpie a long time

Parpie,
Loveliest of animals,
Who's the sweetest kitty
In all of New York City?
How many soft, lovely hairs
Do you have?
How many whiskers,
Of all sizes and lengths?
How do you purr?
What makes your eyes
That incredible blue?
How did your tiny feet
Turn out so perfectly,
Able to run and play so well,
And also touch me so very gently?
How did you get
Such a loving disposition?
How can I be so lucky
To have
You, Parpie the Magnificent,
In my life?
You're one of my major blessings,
One of my greatest sources
Of friendship, pleasure, and peace.
Another reason
For living,
For continuing.

Onslaught

February 11, 1993

Onslaught
Yields tension, insecurity, fear.
Continuing onslaught
Over a long period of time
Increases all of those things,
Moves me closer to collapse
Mentally, emotionally, physically—
Closer to overwhelmed.
Confusion grows,
Multiplying and magnifying my discomforts.

Short-term memory is blunted by,
Among other things,
Distraction, preoccupation
With my physical ordeal.
What do I do at this point?
I can't think of anyone
To call.
Can't think of anyone
I want to tell about this.
What good will it do?
It only takes time
And phone money (for family or friends)
Or taxi money (minister, psychologist).

Sleep and prayer help
More than anything.
Yes, prayer gives me spiritual comfort;
Sleep rests my weary mind.

Breakthroughs

February 11, 1993
Before talking to David K.

Slowly but surely
Tear flow returning
Alleviating burning
And pain in my eye.

Saliva returning
Beginning my mouth's turning
To moist
From cracker-dry.

Skin slowly returning
From itching and burning
To cool and smooth
And irritation-free.

These things
Should break through
My fatigue and discouragement
And bring peace to me.

I Feel Like I'm Going Away

February 15, 1993
After midnight

God bless
Mommy and Daddy dear,
Heavenly Father,
Draw me near.
Amen.

Thank you Mom and Dad
For my Life.

Thank you, Mom,
For chocolate crazy cake after school,
All the clothes you made me,
All the cooking, sewing,
Cleaning, and laundry you did
And taught me to do.
Thank you for all of the Valentine boxes
And Halloween costumes
You made and sent to school with me.
Beyond that, thank you
For my basic education
On becoming a woman.
Thank you for pasties,*
Help with homework,
And the innumerable things
You have helped me with and through
All of my life.

Dad,
Thank you for the hours we spent together
Tending the victory garden,
For taking me to the bank and showing me off,
Giving me baths when I was very little,
Complete with songs and silliness.
Teaching me how to write checks,
Helping me get summer jobs
With your charm (for them)
And caring (for me).

*pass′tees: traditional meat, potato and vegetable pie from Great Britain.

Loving and accepting me
With your quiet, gentle way,
Telling me your stories and jokes (again!).
Mostly, thanks for being so dependable—
Always the same, always loving,
Always there.

You two have led exemplary lives
As providers,
As mates,
As parents,
As citizens.
Vicki and I are so blessed
To have you as
Our mother and father.

I'll miss you both,
But we'll meet again in joy and peace.
I love you forever.

Wider Vision

February 20, 1993
11:00 pm

It seems
There is no return
To narrow view
Once you have developed
A wider vision.
Once moved
To explore the world a little,
With its dazzling variety
Of people, places, and things,
It's simply impossible
Not to be affected,
Challenged, changed, broadened
By what is experienced
During the ventures out.
Life becomes richer,
More interesting, and fun!
Life presents more possibilities
And wonders
Than heretofore have been
Imaginable.
The new information
Just won't fit
In the old framework;
The new stuff
Just won't fit
In the old box.
To celebrate this fact
Is the next natural step.
Thank you,
Creator, giver of this life.
Deepest thanks.

My Cozy Traps

February 20, 1993
Midnight

My cozy traps
Have been in so many places—
Family,
Social convention,
Religion/church,
House in the suburbs,
Urban pad
In the sky over Manhattan,
My denial of reality.
However
It sometimes becomes
Absolutely necessary,
A matter of life and death, really,
To step out of a place
That has become too cozy,
Too familiar, too comfortable,
Too much the same,
Too tight,
Too limited and limiting,
And deal with past and present
Realities.
Perhaps things never were
The way we tried to think of them,
For ourselves or others.
Pretense, self-delusion,
Societal dishonesty,
Self-limitation
Slow us down.
They stunt,
And then begin to suffocate us.

The greatest tragedy in life
Is loss of self,
And all the marvelous potentialities
And precious things
Self can do, experience, and be.
It's hard to understand
Why or how this happens;
There must be more reasons

Than shall ever be known
Or understood.

But daring to be
My true Self
Has required, until recently,
More help and guidance
Than came to me,
More courage
Than I could muster.

Only now am I beginning
To get a glimpse of the real me.
Please, God,
Give me a little more time
To come closer
To what I am capable of
In your world.

Amen.

Growth Includes Upheaval

February 21, 1993
1:00 am

Episodes
Of great mental conflict,
Spiritual conflict,
Religious conflict
Have shaken me,
Deeply upsetting me of late.
I have been thrown back
Into contact with
My earlier stages of
Religion and faith.
Though I am the same in many ways,
In some significant ways
I have changed dramatically;
I am simply not the same person
I was twenty years ago.
This remarkable degree of change
Causes a bit of dismay
Amongst some family members and friends.
It's a shock
To deal with me
In my present state of spirituality.
It is a dramatically different,
Expanded view of life.

So I have been back in touch
With helpers,
Ministers, psychologists,
Spiritual friends and family members,
And now, once again
I am confident, thank Heaven,
Of my spiritual path
And journey.
It is clearer all the time:
There is no significant growth
Without turmoil and upheaval.
I feel a little like
A reptile, growing until
Its too-small skin splits.
A snake wriggles and writhes,
Squirms and struggles

To shed the old, outgrown part of herself,
Freeing herself to become fully
Who she is now.
Another lovely skin that fits
Is already in place.
That is how it is to be growing—
Through work and struggle
A new creature emerges
And can go on,
Renewed and stronger,
To the next part of life.

Everybody Sand Down the Bumps! (A Fantasy)

February 21, 1993
2:00 am

Every valley shall be exalted,
And every mountain and hill made low;
The crooked straight,
And the rough places plain.—LUKE 3:5

These days I'm in an increasing hurry.
Life seems so tenuous!
How long can I last,
Be active, effective,
"Bat it around,"
Going through life
More or less normally?
Though I know the folly of it,
I want the world to get on its horse,
Starting at close range
But stretching to global scale.
Stop cutting down the rain forests!
Stop polluting and desecrating the natural world!
Stop hating and destroying
And engaging in these
Horrendous wars with
Your neighbors!
Stop neglecting and abusing
Yourself, your family,
And others around you!
Communicate, cooperate,
Enfold and include,
Love and nurture!
Build bridges, not bombs!
On every scale,
Let us make the rough places plain.
My energies and time
Are increasingly limited—
I would like to leave the world
A smooth and peaceful place.
We've so much work to do.
Come on everybody,
Let's work together
To sand down the bumps!

Sacred Process—As I See It Now I

March 13, 1993
9:00 pm
Day of "The storm of the century"

Today has given the East Coast
A terrible storm,
Starting in Florida,
With seventeen tornadoes and
Hurricane-strength winds.
Every state from Georgia to Maine
Has been lambasted
With record snows, winds,
Rain and sleet unparalleled
Since "the great storm of '88"—1888!

That is the kind of mental storm
I have begun to experience.
Repeatedly I fight a syndrome
Whereby my mind is going chaotically
At about a thousand miles per hour,
Essentially paralyzing me
Into nearly total ineffectiveness
For the tasks at hand.
I sometimes stand or sit, staring,
While a strange kind of reverie goes on.
I make lists of what I need to do,
And this helps.
But if I mislay the list,
Which happens regularly,
I lose train of thought
And tend to move about
Somewhat aimlessly,
Forgetting what it is
That I've forgotten.
My neurologist tells me
The radiation treatments to my head
Are responsible.
Whatever the cause,
It is extremely discouraging
And upsets me increasingly.
Combined with poor instant recall and
Poor sense of balance,

Maybe it is understandable
That I'm just not very productive at all
Some days.
Add to this the relentlessness
Of my illness at this point,
And considering that I've been
Dealing with it for twenty-seven years,
I guess it's miraculous
That I'm doing as well as I'm doing.

I still see it all
As sacred process,
Of course.
No one ever said
It would be easy.
But I see it all now
With increasing weariness,
Weariness that only deepens
As time goes on.
Maybe I will experience
My approaching death this way—
Ever-increasing weariness.
Perhaps every VHL episode
Will make it easier to at last let go
Of my earthly pleasures
And the people I love
For a while,
And get on with
The next leg
Of my remarkable, difficult,
Holy journey.

Sacred Process—As I See It Now II

March 14, 1993
Sunday, 10:30 am

Everything and its opposite
Tugs and pulls and whirls
Inside my mind.
I don't finish one line of thinking
Without beginning others.
Trains of thought overlap,
Pile up,
Quietly insist,
Clash,
Compete
For my attention
And action
On their behalf.
I am overwhelmed
By a jumble of
Thoughts and images.
Everything imaginable
Besieges my consciousness
With increasing intensity these days.

Maybe that is how
I should measure
My "progress" at this point.
It seems
My increasing suffering
Here and now
Is moving me, very slowly,
Toward comfort and adjustment
To my approaching
New realities.

Sacred Process—As I See It Now III

March 14, 1993
Sunday, 11:00 am

Physical sight dimmed and threatened
Hearing diminished
Partial facial paralysis
Poor sense of balance
Post-radiation-impaired memory,
Knowledge of my disease's progression,
Down several considerable
Body parts.
(I've laughingly said
It turns out they were
Spare parts.)
Pieces of my physical self
Already gone ahead of me
Into the other reality.
With all of this,
I will go on,
Loving life as I live it
With as much gusto and dignity
As I can muster.
Life continues to awe me,
Tickle me,
Thrill me,
And, yes, nurture me.
What more could I ask?
The love affair continues.

Sacred Process—As I See It Now IV

March 14, 1993
Sunday, 11:45 am

My life is beset these days
With the most awesome combination
Of intense perceptions
And experiences.

An image came to me this morning
As I was waking:
Life is a loving, warm, comfy,
Soft and fuzzy big animal,
And I am the very young offspring
Of this magnificent creature.
This animal nuzzles me,
Feeds me,
Washes me,
Plays with me,
Shows me how to survive.
At the end of the day
It snuggles me, and I
Rest and sleep in absolute
Trust, joy, security and contentment
Among the folds of its lovely,
Loving softness and warmth.

What an incredible gift,
This waking image.
So real, so comforting.
Thank you, Lord
For this most recent blessing.

Gifted via TV

March 15, 1993
9:30 am

Yes, there are good things
On television!
I happened upon a program
Called "In Search Of" last night,
An intriguing piece on
"Other Voices,"
Which explored
The sensibilities of plants,
Including ways in which
They relate to and communicate
With all other life forms.
What a message of
Universality!
It truly and concretely points,
I feel, to the interconnectedness
Of everything in the universe:
How everything is affected, moved, changed
By each organism's
Life events.
There are no words to express
My joy at the evidence of
The enormity and complexity
And Oneness of all things.

Crucial Companionship

March 19, 1993
Noon
After an hour on the phone

We must try to remember:
To cope more easily
With life's ups and downs,
There is no substitute
For human contact.
Oh yes, some solitude is
Desirable at times.
But too much of it
Can become depressing,
Causing lethargy, sadness and anxiety.
Loneliness can lead to
Too much concentration on self,
One's maladies, worries and doubts.
Even beloved pets
Cannot fill the need
For the quality of connection
That goes on between
Two caring people.

Getting out
Even to walk among strangers
Is helpful,
As is a pleasant
Telephone conversation.
If you can't,
For some reason,
Have a friend in
For a meal or tea,
Just to drop that friend
A note or letter
Is an amazing help.
Have you noticed, too, that
Having a little company,
By whatever method,
Can have a lovely,
Renewing, healing
Effect?

Sacred Process—As I See It Now V

March 16, 1993
9:00 am
Sitting in the sun with Parpie
at the kitchen table

"We know that in everything
God works for good
With those who love him,
Who are called according to
His purpose."
ROMANS 8:28

Farther along,
I now see
The Process
More thrilling,
More exciting,
More awesome,
More joy-inducing, delightful
Than ever.
It approaches
Rapture.

With Your Love and Peace, Lord

November 11, 1992
morning

With your love and peace, Lord,
Surround us.
With your beauty,
Touch us.
With your Holy Spirit
Please enter and dwell within us
Until we are Spirit-filled
To such an extent
That your goodness
Can emanate from us,
Touching, moving whomever we meet,
Until we become truly aware that
We are a part of
An endlessly expanding evolution:
Your love and peace are
Limitless.

Thank you,
Thank you, Lord.

Amen.

Companion piece to
Invitation

Paintings

Legend

1. *Maria*, oil, 28 x 40, 1989
   This sweet woman, a Russian immigrant, was a model at the National Academy of Design in New York.

2. *Lilly's Basket, Bearing Fruit,* pastel, 15 x 25, 1991
   The subject reflects Lilly herself: a combination of quiet elegance and simplicity.

3. *Willows at Lake Geneva,* pastel, $18\frac{1}{4}$ x 25, 1991
   The site of family vacations in Wisconsin.

4. *Self-Portrait,* pastel, $17\frac{1}{2}$ x 21, 1987
   First pastel self-portrait.

Karen Forsell
1989

1991

Karen Forsell